Up to speed with workflow

How to choose a business process improvement methodology for your organization and measure the positive change

Shruti Bhat PhD, MBA
Certified Lean Six Sigma Black Belt

First Edition

Business Process Management Systems and Continuous Improvement Executive Guide Series.

Published by Shifting Paradigms Publications, Canada.

Copyright

Disclaimer and FTC Notice

The author and publisher of this book have used their best efforts in preparing this work. The information contained in this book has been stated accurately to the best ability of the author and publisher. The information contained in this book is strictly for educational purposes.

The author and publisher make no representation or warranties with respect to the accuracy, contrary interpretations of the subject matter herein, applicability, fitness or completeness of the contents of this book. Therefore, if you wish to apply ideas contained in this book, you are taking full responsibility for your actions. The author and

ISBN 978-0-9937769-2-2

ISBN 978-0-9948255-3-7

ISBN: 978-0-9948255-6-8 (Kindle)

ISBN: 978-0-9948255-7-5 (ePub)

Library and Archives Canada Cataloguing in Publication

Bhat, Shruti, 1967-, author
        Up to speed with workflow : how to choose a business process improvement methodology for your organization and measure the positive change / Shruti Bhat PhD, MBA. -- First edition.

 (Business process management systems and continuous improvement executive guide series) Electronic monograph.
ISBN 978-0-9937769-2-2 (ebook)

        1. Workflow--Management. 2. Organizational change. I. Title.
II. Series: Bhat, Shruti, 1967- Business process management systems
and continuous improvement executive guide series.

HD62.17.B53
2015   658.5'3   C201
5-903285-7

ISBN 978-1-988663-10-4 (Paperback)

Cover Creative Concept & Design by
Macro2Micro Media
Canada

Published By:

ShiftingParadigms
Canada

Dedicated to my wonderful parents

Umesh S. Bhat

and

Shanta U. Bhat

Table of Contents

FREE GIFT

About the author...

SHRUTI U. BHAT, Ph.D, MBA, CLSSBB

Shruti is a Profitability Expert.

Shruti is PhD in Manufacturing Technology, MBA and Certified Lean Six Sigma Black Belt, with more than 1000 successful innovation, business process design and continuous improvement projects delivered to satisfied clients worldwide. She has turned-around failing companies to successful enterprises, helped solve cash-flow problems, improved Operations/ Service levels and PROFITS.

Shruti *specializes* with biotech, engineering, pharmaceuticals, bulk drugs, natural products, foods & beverages, medical devices, chemicals, and cosmetics industry verticals. She works with startups, small to mid-size and growing companies.

Strategic Innovation Management:

Through her customized "ROI strategy design", Shruti provides cutting- edge concepts of Innovation-by- Design to create affordable quality products that are "Tough to copy". She helps clients gain first-mover advantage via *Design-Thinking* based *Lean Innovations* and drives business growth.

Strategic Continuous Improvement:

Shruti's efforts facilitate her clients to reduce operation costs, backorders, variations, product defects and returns. She is an authority with 32 different hi-tech manufacturing technologies, as well as 3D Printing operations.

She designs and drives implementation of eighteen proven business improvement methodologies, such as, Kaizen, 5S, Lean Six Sigma, ISO, JIT, Poka Yoke, Hoshin Kanri, CAPA, TQM, Quality-by-design, Agile. By strategic use of these techniques, she has significantly reduced production cycle times, COGs (cost of goods) and increased operational efficiency.

She has helped build enterprise teams and coached more than 12,000 employees on topics such as DOE, Continuous Improvement, Design Thinking.

Shruti is Chief Operations Officer at Innoworks Inc. a Canadian Management Consulting company with offices in Vancouver, Calgary and Toronto. She has authored 4 books, over 90 publications in peer-reviewed journals and has 25 patents to her credit.

Online & Social media connect:

Website: www.DrShrutiBhat.com
Contact:
http://www.drshrutibhat.com/contact.html
LinkedIn:
https://www.linkedin.com/in/drshrutibhat
Twitter: https://twitter.com/ShrutiUBhat
Google+:
https://plus.google.com/+ShrutiBhat/posts
You Tube:
https://www.youtube.com/user/shrutibhat10
Facebook:
https://www.facebook.com/Innoworks.Inc

About Innoworks ...

Innoworks is a Canadian Management Consulting firm with offices in Vancouver, Calgary and Toronto.

Business success increasingly hinges on a company's ability to leverage tools, new technology, creative concepts to drive innovation, improve operational efficiency and organizational excellence. Advance your business with Innoworks's Design Thinking, Rapid Prototyping, Lean Innovation Quality Improvement, Business Transformation and Continuous Improvement Expert Services.

Innoworks is in the business of helping businesses GROW!

Website: http://www.innoworks.ca/
Video:
https://www.youtube.com/watch?v=g39qYtCG-qI

Preface

Up to speed with workflow- How to choose business process improvement methodology for your organization and measure the positive change, is the third book of "Business process management systems and Continuous Improvement Executive Guide Series".

Businesses in US, Canada or in any country worldwide, are governed by five factors, referred as '5M' umbrella- Man, Money, Machine, Material and Methods.

Methods or *processes*, being the most critical out of the five, as, it alone (to a large extent) determines the consequences of the other 4Ms i.e. Man, Money, Machine and Materials.

For examples, if the *processes* in a company were engaging, then employees would stay committed and contribute positively. 'Machines' would be productive, costs would go down and 'Materials' would be wisely used to generate profitable products, which in turn will help the business thrive, grow and make more money. *Therefore, processes drive a chain reaction.*

Business processes in any organization, can be made more efficient, more effective, and adaptable to changing market and/ or economic needs. However, the biggest problem faced by most companies worldwide, is not its competitors, rather the biggest problems are self-inflicted, that is, created in-house by the management.

Therefore, a step further in this direction is to build *'quality'* and *'profitability'* into business processes.

What will you learn from this book?

This book covers the following topics –

- Introduction to business process improvement lifecycle.

- How to strategically design process improvement initiatives to win campaigns.

- Roadmap to process improvement methodology selection including- base lining, change management, organizing business processes within an organization, identifying business process problem areas, various process improvement techniques and process improvement methodologies.

- Decision matrix for selecting process improvement methodology for your workplace.

- Action plan- for doing methodology implementation right!

- Qualifying 'new' business process and efficiency measurement metrics.

- Maintaining 'continued' operational excellence with the 'new' process.

- Illustrative examples of process improvement methodology recommendations for-

  - Healthcare organization.

  - Facility management and maintenance department of manufacturing organizations.

  - IT department of non-profits, technology companies and manufacturing industries.

  - Customer service departments of service organizations.

- Frequently asked questions and tips to maximize output from business process improvement campaigns.

Who should read this book?

This book presents practical ways to build and improve business processes, and assists professionals whether they are learning the basics

of business process improvement (or continuous improvement), planning their first improvement project, or evangelizing process oriented thinking throughout their organization.

This book is for Agile entrepreneurs, Startups, Leaders, QA (Quality Assurance) managers, Management consulting professionals, Production supervisors, Manufacturing heads, CEOs, Directors and Managers involved in decision-making, directing their organization's sustainability, profitability, and expansion.

If you want some new and effective ideas for improving your organization's efficiency, then this self-help, business management book is for you.

This book is also for professionals who are interested in making a career change and wish to embrace business process management (bpm) role.

This book simplifies business improvement methodologies, gives sequential steps to facilitate selecting a business process improvement, which is *right* for your organization, helps you understand the principles that drive business improvement and give your career the boost it needs!

This book helps executives; professionals improve organizational performance in their role as a Management Consultant, Business Analyst, Continuous Improvement, or Process Management Expert.

This book is not body of knowledge (BoK) for a certification exam. Rather, this book is for all "business readers" who wish to apply business improvement methodologies to their work place in most beneficial, effective and practical ways.

This book is also for graduate students in the process of stepping into the industrial world- be it manufacturing or a service industry.

This book helps you learn the various methods by which you can improve your company's business processes, which in turn would help your individual career growth.

It has brought me lot of joy in creating this book, series and I hope you enjoy reading it too.

As it is often said, "All good begins with gratitude and thanks".

I take this first step. Thanks to my lovely parents and my sister Sandhya, for their mammoth support. I also thank them for encouraging me with this *motto* 'Continuously be a better individual and be good with whatever you are doing'.

Thanks to my friends and colleagues who worked with me, tirelessly, on business improvement programs- Together, we have bettered many businesses!

Lastly, but not the least, a big thanks to the divine, universe for bringing the good to me and for investing the intellect in me, to express my thoughts and seep-in, this joy of writing.

Shruti Bhat

Introduction

Management of key business processes is of utmost importance to becoming a high performing organization, as they are the means to executing business strategies, by aligning process results with business goals.

Do the right thing for the customer and the customer will do the right thing for you. - Dr. Joseph Juran

As customer needs change frequently, one has to monitor them continuously and this is the fundamental basis for 'Business process improvement' and 'Continuous improvement'. Those who learn this outperform their competitors because they have a much better understanding of their customers.

Business process improvement drives substantial bottom-line increases, customer satisfaction, ultimately accelerating the company's revenue cycle. In today's highly dynamic economies, the ones who do not get this mantra eventually have two choices- they get it or they go out.

However, the biggest problem faced by most companies worldwide, is not its competitors. Rather the biggest problems are self-inflicted, that is, created in-house by the management. So how does a company choose the right business process improvement methodology to implement at their organization?

This would depend on what problem prevails in the organization, that one is trying to solve and why. For example- is there a design issue? A process issue? A defect issue? A variation issue? Or a combination of them.

The success of process improvement directly depends on the process improvement methodology selected to bring on the positive change.

It is equally true that choosing a *correct* process improvement methodology is critical and extremely challenging. This in turn depends on the 'Process improvement lifecycle' comprising of following steps-

Step 1: Base lining.

Step 2: Identify critical 'process improvement' implementation success factors.

Step 3: Organize and centrally locate processes.

Step 4: Standardize processes spread across multiple functions and business units.

Step 5: Re-design ineffective or in-efficient processes.

Step 6: Eliminate work-around or duplicate steps.

Step 7: Automate processes wherever possible.

Step 8: Identify and apply metrics and KPI (key performance indicators).

Step 9: Cross-train employees.

'Identification' of process improvement methodology stems out of information gathered from steps 1 to 3, while the success of 'methodology implementation' is dependent on steps 4 to 9.

'Business process improvement methodology selection' involves two phases– 'methodology identification' and 'methodology implementation'

This book highlights salient details about "*How to choose a business process improvement methodology for your organization and measure the positive change*". Further, in the book we will dive into which methodologies might be appropriate for different industry verticals, different processes and diverse types of companies, as well as few important frequently asked questions.

Coming up in the next chapter- *Potential success factors to winning process improvement campaigns...*

Winning process improvement campaigns?

To meet success with business process improvement initiatives, one should seek answers to following basic questions-

i.   What 'change' objective(s) are we trying to achieve?

ii. How are we measuring the 'change' i.e. how will we know that a 'change' is an 'improvement'?

iii. What 'changes' should we make that will result in an 'improvement'?

Keys to successful business process improvement campaigns include-

i.   **Customer-centric approach:** There should be unrelenting focus on the customer, whether internal of external customer and their needs.

ii. **Buy-in from top management,** to bring forth the culture change i.e. senior leadership support.

iii. **Risk hesitancy:** Management should reduce fear of failure, rewards risks that do

11

not pay off in an equivalent way to risks that do pay off.

iv. **Road map:** A crystal-clear vision. There should be no ambiguity about what the business process improvement project is trying to achieve. Not having a clear vision, focus and strategic road map to deploy process improvement methodology leads to 'no-where'.

v. **Plain spoken and extensive communication:** Simple communication, no jargon. Communication is important while developing a culture of business improvement because it allows employees to feel confident in asking questions as they learn new skills. They should know whom they can ask the questions to and should feel comfortable asking those questions. In addition, it is necessary for anticipations to be expressed as clearly as possible and repeated frequently, so that employees are reminded.

By using a variety of assessment tools, such as tests, observations or reviews, one can assess employee's improvement. Assessing improvement should be done frequently in order to ensure that individuals are on the right track. It is also a good gauge of knowing whether learning sessions should be increased or if other skills should be focused-on instead.

vi.   Culture change:

Culture change sets in easily, when employees 'see' benefits vs 'being told' about benefits. Quick wins gain employee trusts.

Perhaps one of the most important ways of developing business improvement culture in an organization is to let the employees know the significance of their contributions to the goal.

Employees ought to know their contributions are greatly appreciated and respected. Questions, feedback and ideas are just some of the many ways that employees can contribute to continuous improvement programs.

Additionally, employees need to be trained along the way, so that the status quo of 'Improved business performance' is consistent. The frequency of training session would vary based on the methodology/ skill involved.

Initiating a culture of 'business process improvement' in an organization means that employees are constantly learning, improving and adding to the main goal of the organization. It helps all individuals involved to move in the same desirable direction and meet goals in an organized manner.

Developing such a culture often relies on the "business improvement facilitator's" ability to communicate, share ideas, evaluate the current scenario and overcome obstacles.

vii. **Include 'best' people on the process improvement team** and the rates of succeeding are exponentially increased. 'Best' people could be either consistent high performers or grass-root members i.e. front liners executing the process.

viii. **Actively manage process improvement campaigns:** Process improvement leadership is a full-time responsibility and not a part-time function.

Define a business improvement facilitator/ leader, who actively directs the project, has the ability to deal with a complex variety and large number of business issues.

Generally, issues are highlighted by management or aggrieved employee(s) and it will be up to the business improvement expert to identify the underlying problem and advise ways to solve them successfully.

ix. **Realistic approach:** Different people transition through change differently. Top management/ Executive team must exhibit maturity and realize that not everyone within the organization is going to move at the same pace.

The next chapter presents *Roadmap to selecting business process improvement methodology ...*

Shruti Bhat

Roadmap to methodology selection

This chapter presents *Roadmap to selecting business process improvement methodology* and comprises of following sub-sections -

- Base lining.
- Getting organizational change right.
- Organizing business processes in an organization.
- Identifying business process 'problem areas' in a manufacturing or service organization.
- Various process improvement techniques.
- Various process improvement methodologies.
- 'Decision matrix' for selecting process improvement methodology.

Base-lining i.e. mapping existing business processes- Coming up, in the next chapter ...

Base-lining

To initiate business process improvement campaign in your organization, one has to begin by taking stock of the 'As- is' position, fix a goal and then build procedures to attain that goal in a systematic and meaningful manner.

It is all about 'methods' that are needed to get profitable business results, consistently! Base lining kicks off with three fundamental questions-

- Is there a problem?

- Is the problem worth solving i.e. what happens if nothing is done?

- Does the problem affect the business's bottom line?

Expanding on the above, we define whether there truly is a problem; or whether wrong problems are being addressed. For example, if a customer service department has work overload, it is imperative to investigate whether this overload is due to poor work efficiency of the employees in that department or because of high rates of product recalls or high rates of product returns.

Once the problem is identified, the next questions to find answers for are- Is the problem worth solving or just living with i.e. what happens if nothing is done? Whether the problem affects the business's brand image, customer goodwill, top-line, bottom-line? Responses to these queries brings forth clarity of the problem, its scope, nature and magnitude.

Next step then, is to identify existing process flow. For example, what do we (i.e. the business) do? How do we do it? What starts our process? What ends our process? Does our product or service comply with any 'acceptance criteria' desired by our customers, regulators, etc.? A strategic and structured 'pre-assessment' finds true answers to all of the questions effectively.

When pre-assessment is not done for a project, that project may not see success at all. In fact, a study of 'failed' projects revealed improper pre-assessment as the number one cause for failure.

> *Process improvement projects fail not because of improper execution. They fail because either pre-assessment was not done correctly or the improvement methodology selected was incorrect.*

For every business improvement project, irrespective of its size, time invested through pre-assessment will go a long way towards avoiding projects, which actually should not have started and succeeding in the ones, which do need to start.

In all business processes however bad, always some process work while some do not. 'As-is' process design allows to prevent breaking processes that actually work.

In addition, it gives complete picture of a company's situation, facilitates finding out the root causes for the scenario, suggest ways of rectifying the problem(s) and gives insights into choosing process improvement methodology best suited for the organization.

Broadly, there are three main benefits of doing a pre-assessment-

i.   Helps to choose the most appropriate process improvement methodology. Applying correct methodology will save huge costs of implementation to the company.

ii.   Not doing 'As-is' status can provide great opportunities to reinvent past mistakes, since nobody knows why the mistakes got committed in the first place.

iii.   Implementing a new methodology without doing 'As-is' status might create a process that generates new mistakes, which may not be evident until it is too late.

*Nothing can be established
without norms, standards or tools.*

– Old Chinese proverb

Several tools available for conducting 'pre-assessment' or base-lining include- Flow charts, process benchmarking, value stream analysis, Ishikawa diagrams, histograms, scatter plots, Pareto charts, process mapping, etc.

Flow Charts

Flow charts are diagrams used to show various stages of a process that makes it easy for those viewing the chart to understand and view the entire process. It is a beneficial tool for exhibiting various process flows in an organization as well as the respective roles these processes play. In addition, flow charts provide concise documentation regarding the stages of a specific job or project.

Process Benchmarking

Benchmarking defines and compares a business against others, permits understanding where the business stands and how can it be advanced. It typically compares the practices used in one's business in comparison to others to find out the standards or practices, which are most applicable, and helps to improve overall performance.

Value stream analysis

Value stream analysis records, evaluates and enhances information flow that is necessary to produce a service or product. This technique solely uses pen and paper to gain insight and understanding of the movement of information or materials through the value stream that contributes to the production of services and/or products.

Ishikawa diagrams

Ishikawa diagrams also known as fishbone diagrams depict the causes of individual events and the connection between the events. These diagrams are effective to pinpoint the cause of a specific quality or business problem to fix the issue.

Histograms

Histograms give a rough assessment of the probability of a source of a problem. It shows the occurrences of observations that occur amongst the subject's focus point.

Pareto charts

Pareto charts contain line graphs and bars to represent data graphically. It is a method of finding out where the sources of defects arise; pinpoint the source of largest reoccurring defect and its frequency. Pareto charts are easy to understand due to their simple, but detailed mode of visual presentation.

Process mapping

Process mapping is a tool used to show workflow in a visual manner. It is an organization tool for communicating ideas and planning within businesses. The main aspects of process mapping include inputs, outputs, stages, decision points and functions. The information made available through process mapping allows those who view it to gain insight into steps, which are paired with brief explanations.

The above tools when used singly or in combination provide vital baseline data that is-

Scope of the problem, its nature and magnitude, potential success factor and/or de-accelerators to process improvement campaigns, which business process improvement methodology to choose to bring on the positive change, route of successful methodology implementation etc.

The definition of insanity is doing the same thing over and over again, but expecting different results. – Albert Einstein

---

My book entitled 'Continuous Improvement Tools- 30 Proven tools to drive Profitability, Quality and Operational Effectiveness in Manufacturing & Service Industry' discusses thirty vital tools, essential to meet success with your Continuous Improvement campaigns.

Coming up in the next chapter- *Getting organizational change right*!

This chapter discusses various change management models for seeking success with process improvement campaigns ...

Change management models

Driving organizational change is an important activity vital for successful implementation of business improvement methodology. Organizational change therefore, must be a structured approach to ensure that changes are smooth, implemented successfully to achieve consistent, lasting results and make the organization more efficient, effective and profitable.

The success of change management depends on the accuracy of the baseline data (discussed in previous chapters), employee motivation levels, project management aptitude and leadership qualities of the change facilitator as well as the 'toughness' of the process improvement methodology itself. Hence, using appropriate 'change management' technique is the name of the game.

Successful change management involves following stages-

   i.   Determine the need for change.

   ii. Develop a case for change including alternatives, risks and resources implications.

   iii. Communicating the vision for change.

   iv. Developing a strategy for change.

v. Managing the change process.

There are several change management techniques available. However, I have found Kotter's 8-step change model, Lewin change management model, ADKAR model and McKinsey 7S model, to be not only extremely successfully but also, versatile across several industry verticals.

Kotter's 8-step change model

The model comprises of-

Step 1: Create urgency for change.

Step 2: Form a powerful coalition.

Step 3: Create a vision for change.

Step 4: Communicate the vision.

Step 5: Remove obstacles.

Step 6: Create short-term wins.

Step 7: Build on the change.

Step 8: Secure the changes firmly within corporate culture.

Lewin's change management model

The model comprises of-

Step 1: Unfreeze, that is break down the existing status quo.

Step 2: Transition after change.

Step 3: Refreeze, which means, making sure that the 'changes' get used all the time and that they are incorporated into everyday business.

ADKAR change management model

The model suggests that 'change' requires managing five key goals-

Goal 1: **A**wareness of the need to change.

Goal 2: **D**esire to participate and support the change.

Goal 3: **K**nowledge of how to change (and what the change looks like).

Goal 4: **A**bility to implement the change on a routine basis.

Goal 5: **R**einforcement to keep the changes consistent.

McKinsey 7S change management model

McKinsey's model examines an organization as a collection of business flows with a critical link between operational drivers and strategic success.

Apropos this model, seven core elements often referred as Seven Ss are needed to evaluate businesses, and find out what processes are effective and which are not. In order to gain advantage, businesses must focus on all seven elements simultaneously, since they are inter related. Any change to one of the seven elements will have a ripple effect over the remaining six elements.

7S model includes-

S1: *Strategy*, refers to the proposal that is created to sustain and improve business processes against its competitors.

S2: *Structure*, is the approach that the organization is arranged concerning ranking and how issues should be reported and to whom.

S3: *Systems*, incorporates the daily processes that employees are required to participate in in order to complete the task.

S4: *Shared values*, otherwise known as superordinate goals, are the company's key values that are evident in the culture of the corporation and general work approach.

S5: *Staff*, refers to all of the company's employees and what they are capable of.

S6: *Skill*, implies the skills and proficiencies of the company's staff.

S7: *Style*, refers to the entire spectrum of corporate governance.

A big advantage of the 7S model is that, it is applicable to any industry, type or size of teams. On the other hand, it has a major limitation as well as. That is, unless appropriately handled, this model can exhibit higher failure rates.

Next phase of business process improvement campaign is to clearly define and express expectations to employees. For example- it is common for expectations to include punctual employees, attendance at gatherings, timely completion of project milestones, timely submission of project data etc.

One of the most important ways of bringing on business process improvement in an organization is to let the employees know their significance to the goal.

Employees ought to be aware of the fact that their contributions are greatly appreciated and respected. Questions, feedback and ideas are just some of the many ways that employees can contribute to business improvement program

Using a variety of assessment tools, such as tests, observations or reviews, can assess employee's improvement.

Assessing improvement should be done frequently in order to make sure that individuals are on the right track. It is also a good gauge of knowing whether learning sessions should be increased or if other skills should be focused on instead.

Tip 1: Selecting appropriate change model is vital for successful business process improvement campaign.

Tip 2: Ideal change model for an organization would be dependent on the size of organization, depth & extent of prevailing organizational politics, the types & number of business process 'problem areas' and the business improvement technique.

The next step in the roadmap to choosing process improvement methodology is- *Organizing and centrally locating all business and non-business processes*- Coming up in the next chapter...

Process improvement methodology metrics

The whole purpose of a business is to grow and make money. The whole purpose of a non-business (for example- charities, governments) is to grow and meet budget.

Business processes prevail throughout all organizations be it 'for-profit' or 'non-profit'. Additionally, these processes prevail at all levels within the organization.

Business processes briefly describe the chain of events that are involved in an activity or a group of activities. The number of key cross-functional business processes used within an organization will depend on the nature of the organization, the manner in which its management has structured these processes and the personnel responsible to conduct these processes.

Business processes in product (and/or service) based entities can be broadly classified as – *Delivery and Support processes.*

1. *Delivery processes:*
   Delivery processes are the processes that a customer faces. For example, type of product and/ or product mix, product quality, 'newness' or differentiating features of the product, extent of customer's needs

met by the product, how easily can a customer access or buy the product, how affordable is the product to a customer, what level of after-sales service or product information is provided to a customer etc.

2. **Support processes:**
Support processes are the processes required to sustain the delivery function.

For example- Are you a manufacturing or service organization? How do you recruit, develop & manage your talent pool? What infrastructure do you provide your employees to bring out quality products consistently? How do you choose your product range? What is your product lifecycle management strategy? How do you decide to make/ buy an intermediate necessary for your manufacturing line? How dependable are your vendors, financers, inventory, supply chain & logistics systems? How do you ensure against payment defaults? What are your risk assessment & mitigation modalities? Does your business belong to a regulated industry? What are your guidelines for 'go/ no-go' decisions for entering new markets or industry verticals? Etc.

The fundamental step towards organizing and centrally locating business processes (for improvement) is to define and identify 'key' business processes and their 'problem areas'. So how do we do that?

'Key' business processes are logically grouped related to tasks and activities, independent of the organization's structure, which utilize the resources of the organization to produce specific results.

Coming up, in the next chapter- *25 frequently occurring 'key' business processes with associated 'problem areas' in a manufacturing or service organization...*

Shruti Bhat

Commonly found areas of business processes inefficiency

If you do not know what your problem is, all solutions are bad.

Every organization be it manufacturing or service based, irrespective of its industry vertical, broadly has 25 key business processes (some or all of which might need improvement) and include the following-

i. Main technology in business/ operation process.

ii. Housekeeping and building maintenance.

iii. Team collaboration and conflict management.

iv. Organogram: Strategic rationalizing and integration of different departments within an organization.

v. Quality assurance system, zero defect identification tools, quality policy.

vi. Out sourcing partners/ suppliers/ vendor management.

vii. Production/ work place facility design and EHS compliance.

viii. Product distribution logistics and on time deliveries.

ix. Feedback loop of customer comments.

x. Value chain & Customer conversion rate.

xi. Machinery design & automation.

xii. Reducing machinery down time (cleaning, breakdowns, setups, changeovers, idling) and manufacturing scheduling.

xiii. Minimizing / eliminating reworks, work in process (WIP).

xiv. Minimizing / eliminating product returns.

xv. Product / company marketing and brand building.

xvi. Economic order quantities (EOQ) and inventory management.

xvii. Batch vs Continuous production process.

xviii. Human resource training and continuous development.

xix. Financial health of the business and its tenacity.

xx. Fluidity of the enterprise to adapt to dynamic business environment and offer competitive advantage.

xxi. Time management practices.

xxii. Controlling utilities and overheads.

xxiii. Information technology/ ERP systems.

xxiv. Employee recruitment, empowerment and turnover rate.

xxv. Innovation, knowledge management and intellectual property management.

Business processes work best when there is input, support and ideas contributed from various people that are involved in the organization.

Tip: Therefore, any modification or improvement in business processes is possible only, when people within the organization make business process improvement as their ultimate 'goal'.

This goal can be achieved via three techniques- *Breakthrough improvement, Streamlined improvement and Continuous improvement.*

Coming up! In the next chapter- *Business improvement techniques...*

Business process improvement techniques

In the prior century, business growth was more or less survival of the fittest. In today's times, this is not true- despite the poor economy.

Every business can survive if:

You can accurately find your purpose of existing in the market i.e. find your niche and be constantly adapting your business processes to match your business needs i.e. re-shape quickly, as needed.

– Shruti Bhat

Three main types of business process improvement techniques have been found to be extremely effective in managing, expanding and /or transforming businesses. They are – Breakthrough improvement, Streamlined improvement and Continuous improvement.

Breakthrough improvement is a methodology that incorporates vital improvements to the main areas of business. It is a quicker and more intense

41

method of process improvement. Long-standing and rigorous problems can be solved via Breakthrough improvement.

Streamlined improvement refers to the improvement of a process by reducing and/or shortening the number of steps within a process, in order to lower its intricacy. Streamlined improvement is beneficial since it helps cut back on costs, uses time more effectively and efficiently, as well as improves supervisory observance.

Continuous improvement focuses on undergoing small improvements that take place over a period of time. These increments allow for less disruption to the organization and allow individuals to perform necessary tasks on the agenda in steady and continual stages.

Continuous improvement does not have a huge effect on the organization, though the effects of the improvement tend to stick longer. Many organizations find that, performing small continual improvements has a profound effect in the long run.

Out of the three types of business process improvement techniques, Continuous improvement is often preferred, since the small changes end up adding more 'value' than that offered via Breakthrough or Streamlined improvement.

Breakthrough and Continuous improvement methods use PDCA (Plan-Do-Check-

Act) sequence. Organizations can benefit from using both Continuous and Breakthrough improvement techniques.

Continuous as well as Breakthrough improvement can have a better chance of working properly if- both data and facts are used, individuals are involved & encouraged to find solutions and standard operating methods are established & implemented.

Another possibility is for organizations to perform a *series* of Breakthrough improvements that allow individuals to progressively make continual improvements in their everyday work life.

Organizations that choose to implement this method often reach more desirable results than those that choose just Continuous or Breakthrough improvement. Introducing process automation can further augment effectiveness of the process improvement methodology.

Selection of process improvement technique depends on the circumstances and the desired outcome.

In addition, the chosen technique(s) should be able to weed out un-required processes, redesign inefficient & in-effective processes as well as eliminate 'work-around or duplicate' processes.

Coming up in the next chapter- *Various business process improvement methodologies...*

Business process improvement methodologies

Some of the promising and time tested business process methodologies include- Lean, Theory of constraints, Balanced Score Card, Pareto 80/20 principle, Six Sigma, Just-in-time (JIT), Kaizen, Total Quality Management (TQM), Capability Maturation Model Integration (CMMI), Quality-by-design(QbD), CAPA, Raci matrix, Agile, Scrum, Hoshin Kanri, Jidoka, Poka Yoke, Juran's quality management, ISO, Lean Six Sigma etc.

Each of the above-referred methodologies have their respective application scope, merits, demerits, and limitations. The same have not been covered here, as the topic is vast and demands an independent presentation. My book entitled "Business process improvement for manufacturing and service industry' discusses eighteen such methodologies in great depth.

In addition, one needs to have thorough information about the business model of the company and 'know-how' of different methodologies available in order to make a good selection.

By and large all business process improvement methodologies (be it for a manufacturing or a service based company) employ the PDCA- Plan, Do, Check, Act cycle or

DMAIC- Define, Measure, Analyze, Improve, Control cycle.

Further, it is not only for line managers but also for managers at all levels within an organization to be aware of 'what needs to change and how'. Additionally, every decision maker and doer have to chip in his or her share of activity to diligently paint this huge canvas of business process change.

Tip 1: To achieve this, it is imperative that each employee, vendor and everyone associated with the 'support' of the business to understand his/ her role.

Tip 2: There has to be a metrics of measuring this role. Establish standard operating procedure for performance measurements - How will it be done? Who will do it? How often to make the measurements?

You cannot manage what you cannot measure. Only what gets measured, gets improved. – Dr. W.E. Deming

---

Tip 3: Identify responsible people and collect data. For example, for a procurement department, an important data could be number of on-time deliveries by vendors per month. This data is easy to gather and involves one or perhaps two departments. However, the situation becomes complex in case 'overhead burden rate' must be determined for the organization wherein raw data has to be collected from every department within the organization and assessed by accountants, budget experts!

By now, an important question must have crossed your mind-

There is so much available, so how do I choose which methodology is FIT for my organization?

Next chapter presents- *Decision matrix to choose a business process improvement methodology that is* **right** *for your organization.* Coming up!

'Decision matrix' for selecting methodology

Presented herein, is *'Business process improvement methodology determination matrix'* I created. This decision matrix has tremendously helped me to accurately identify appropriate business process improvement methodology for various industry sectors to bring desired positive results.

Steps to use the methodology determination decision matrix-

Step 1- Examine the business of the company. Define key people, key customers and key stages of the business. Enlist the types of products and services offered by the company. Analyze demand peaks. Review documentation of work practices.

Step 2- Evaluate company culture, probable obstacles and employee resistance quotient.

Step 3- Discuss with the management regarding the budget, resources and period available to bring forth the change.

Step 4- Identify the business problem area(s) and classify it using picture below.

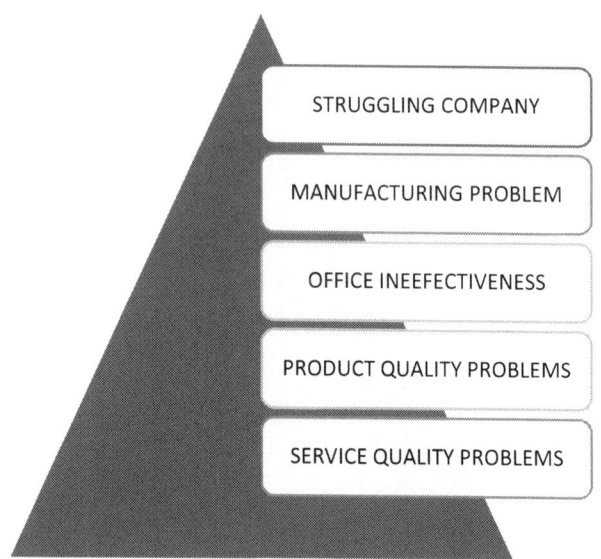

TYPES OF BUSINESS PROBLEMS

Step 5- Based on type of the business problem, select appropriate business process improvement methodology using the recommendations below-

For struggling company improvement, applicable methodologies include- Lean, Balanced scorecard, Just-in-time, Six Sigma, CMMI, Hoshin Kanri, Lean Six Sigma.

For manufacturing problem improvement, applicable methodologies include- Lean, 5S+8D, Just-in-time, Total quality management (TQM),

Kaizen, Six Sigma, ISO, Quality by design + CAPA, Lean +Jidoka, Lean Six Sigma.

For Office ineffectiveness improvement, applicable methodologies include- Lean, 5S, Balanced scorecard, Lean Six Sigma, Pareto principle.

For Product quality problem improvement, applicable methodologies include- Lean, Kaizen, TQM, Quality by design + CAPA, Six Sigma, ISO, Quality by design + 8D, Poka Yoke, Juran principle.

For Service quality problem improvement, applicable methodologies include- Lean, Balanced scorecard, Lean Six Sigma, Pareto principle, 8D + CAPA, Juran principle.

Step 6- Enlist all business processes. Create a list of key business processes or all processes in need of correction. Based on available 'Process understanding' and 'Process control', classify them into four quadrants using picture below-

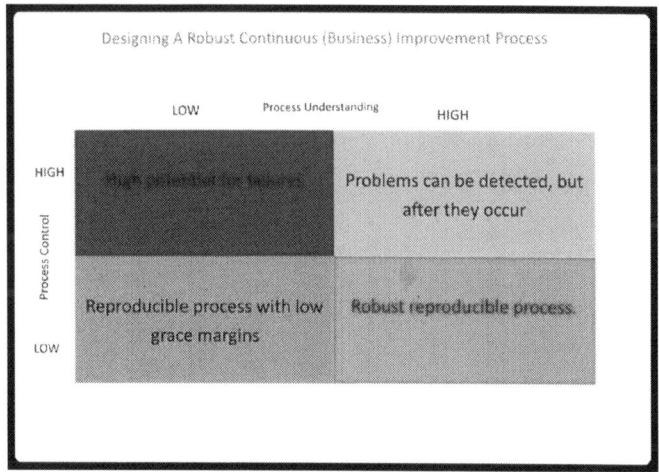

Tip 1: Selection of business improvement methodology candidate largely depends on the number of processes falling in each quadrant. More the number of process in 'red' quadrants difficult the challenge.

Tip 2: I have applied this decision matrix for over eighteen years to different industry verticals and different sizes of organizations, such as-startups, mid-sized, large organizations and multi-locational businesses. I have found the matrix to be extremely versatile, rugged and resourceful.

Variety of business process improvement methodologies, all seem to be the best, can leave any process improvement professional at a loss to decide which is best for their organization. Scoring methodologies therefore, facilitates the selection endeavor.

7-point metrics for finalizing business process improvement methodology-

Rank order the chosen 'candidate' business improvement methodologies using the *7-point metrics*, comprising of-

i. Total cost of business improvement campaign.

ii. Total net financial benefits from process improvement efforts. These include- NPV, payback period, profit estimates, return on investment.

iii. Middle and senior management satisfaction with business processes.

iv. Number of audit findings associated with process inadequacies.

v. Workforce satisfaction with business improvement efforts.

vi. Customer satisfaction with the impact of business improvement efforts.

vii. Percentage of workforce educated about business improvement methodology.

The next step in-line is to implement this chosen methodology successfully.

Tip 1: Always choose the ideal suited methodology. Keep a budgeted version as backup.

Tip 2: Depending upon the number and type of problematic business processes, a strategic combination of two or three methodologies may be needed, to gain the desired breakthrough success quickly, effectively and with a faster rate of return.

Coming up, in the next chapter- *Action plan- Doing implementation right*!

Implementing process improvement strategy correctly?

Regardless of business process improvement methodology selected, i.e. Lean, Six Sigma etc., there are five stages of successful methodology implementation, namely- Model, Deploy, Execute, Monitor and Analyze.

Stage1: Model

The initial phase of business process improvement involves mapping existing process and creating a 'Model'. This model acts as a representative for whatever is necessary in the situation. For example, if focus were on Earth as a whole, then a globe could be used as a model representative. During 'Model' phase, a diagram is created and the goal is clearly outlined. In addition, details for conceptualizing the various stages of the process and its most vital steps documented.

Stage 2: Deploy

Second stage, is 'Deploy'. Here critical activities to be measured are identified. Deploy stage uses the model to expand ideas and come up with a specific list of details. Important details to include during this stage may involve rules and instructions.

55

Using the same example of the Earth-globe model, this stage would develop a map that clearly outlines the route required to go between point A and point B. Decisions are made during deploy stage to select appropriate one or more business improvement methodologies for the organization.

Stage 3: Execute

'Execute' stage interprets the details that are developed during the deploy stage in order to create a workflow from start to finish. This stage creates various tasks and distributes the ideas to the appropriate departments, people or systems depending on the process. It provides enough detail for each person involved to understand their requirements and to fulfill their specific duties, without having to worry about every detail of the entire process.

Example, for a procurement department, an important data could be number of on-time deliveries by vendors per month. This data is easy to gather and involves one or perhaps two departments. However, the situation becomes complex in case 'overhead burden rate' has to be determined for the organization wherein raw data has to be collected from every department within the organization and approved by accountants.

Stage 4: Monitor

The fourth phase, known as the 'Monitor' phase measures performance. Here performance measurement methods and metrics are established. For example- Standard operating procedures stating- How to do performance measurements? Who will do it? How often to make the measurements? During this stage, it is easy to see the various problems or issues involved and to fine-tune the details in order to improve the entire process.

Stage 5: Analyze

'Analyze' phase uses the data retrieved from the entire previous four stages from start to finish. It typically uses data gathered during 'Execute' phase as a starting point to statistically calculate and evaluate data, establish trends, identify statistically significant or insignificant variations, compare actual performance to agreed goals, establish if any corrective actions are necessary and design an 'action plan' to implement changes.

Details typically covered during this stage include- removal of tasks, increasing data retrieval methods, replacing manual stages with automated ones wherever needed/ affordable and improving report/ outputs. The goal of this stage is to figure out what changes can be beneficial to the entire business process.

In addition, it is equally important to assess and establish- are new goals needed? For example-extensive scope change in a business process will necessitate a goal change and possible alternation of performance metrics.

Further, every 'good' process eventually becomes a 'bad' process, as no process stays effective forever in the face of change, such as-customer needs change, technologies change, government policies change, competition changes and what used to be a 'high level performing' process, becomes a poor one and it is time to replace the formerly good process with a new one. Every process cycle should have this capacity of identification, in-built in its charter.

A common question that arises at this point is- "We've designed and executed a business improvement strategy, now what next?"

Tip: The success of business improvement implementation is dependent on successful completion of 'model-deploy-execute-monitor-analyze' stages.

Once, a business process improvement methodology is executed, it needs to be qualified, optimized and validated for efficiency and effectiveness.

The next step is – *Qualifying 'new' business process and evaluating efficiency via metrics-*Coming up …

Shruti Bhat

Methodology evaluation

Business process qualification implies the action that is required in order to verify whether the improved process actually does what it was planned to do. Process qualification helps to determine whether the 'changes' are effective and if the 'new' business process should be continued in use.

One of the many goals of business process qualification is to find out if there are any potential defects in the improved process. This is vital in order to prevent or minimize any potential negative effects on the business such as- overall revenue, customer dissatisfaction, product/ service errors, delivery back orders and the costs/ losses that go along with it etc.

When undergoing business process qualification, business processes are monitored and evaluated at each stage by collecting data. This is done in order to ensure that the stages are being executed in the ideal way and that they are being performed in a way that they should be. Should a problem arise, the information can be immediately circulated to appropriate departments to schedule a repair.

The qualification study can be performed during various stages of a process, such as project, periodic or continuous basis.

'Project basis' entails that the business process qualification is performed once 'new' business improvement methodology is implemented. 'Periodic basis' refers to the use of business process qualification on a monthly or annual basis.

'Continuous basis' business process qualification is when organizations need to assess and confirm the abilities to use their procedures in the near future, or instantaneously. Furthermore, business process qualification may be done manually or automated using software.

Once the 'new' business process is qualified, it needs to be optimized, meaning to choose the best solution (process pathway) from a group of possible solutions. The idea of process optimization is to create a product or service functioning at its optimal level by applying methods, systems and decisions that support it.

Business Process Optimization- The main goal of business process optimization is to make an organization run more efficiently. Various statistical experimental designs such as Latin square, Factorial designs etc. may be used to conduct process optimization.

Generally, two main optimization techniques - Simultaneous or Sequential methods are used. The Simultaneous method allows 'new' process performance evaluation to continue throughout optimization. While, Sequential method requires all process performance evaluations be completed before initiating process optimization.

Tip 1: It often requires quite a bit of experimenting in order to find the best results that cater to providing the best products or services (along with noting the edge of failure).

Tip 2: Too much and unnecessary data gets confusing, leads to analysis-paralysis and in fact, is counterproductive. Type and extent of data collected, should be explicitly defined before collection, in order for it to remain meaningful.

After optimizing the business process, the final step is to evaluate its performance, in terms of- its ease of operation and positive impact on the business.

Measuring success of business process improvement methodology implementation is an elaborate process, comprising of- evaluating business process effectiveness, business process efficiency and metrics measurement.

Implementing new business processes is a large step and requires a lot of communication with employees and sometimes retraining as well. After all implementation stages are complete, it is vital to review the changes and to continue to use the 'new' business process to achieve greater effectiveness.

It is not always essential for organizations to undergo a complete makeover since increasing effectiveness may be done in increments. Once, the effectiveness of the 'new' business process has been established, the next step is evaluating its efficiency. This is an important requirement in order to declare the new (improved) business process to be routinely functional.

For business process efficiency to be successful, there needs to be constant monitoring and assessment of various situations in order to find out what is working and what is not.

Ideas or procedures that do not advance the company, or severely hinder it, should be un-emotionally scrapped.

Business performance improvement measurement uses metrics to monitor and keep records of all aspects of the process. Some key attributes of an ideal metrics are:

i. Reflects the customers' needs as well as that of the organization.

ii. Provides an agreed upon basis for decision-making.

iii. Is unbiased, simple to understand, time-tested and validated.

iv. Has wide applicability.

v. Is precise in interpreting results.

vi. Is economical to apply.

To give more clarity on the subject, presented here are some examples of commonly used metrics by different industries such as sales, financial industries, online marketing, airlines and call center services.

Metric used by financial industries to evaluate the efficiency of an organization could be, by their ability to deal with last-minute liabilities. Sales industries use metrics in order to measure their goals met in a designated space of time (for example sales per month, quarter etc.) and use that measurement in comparison with the overall goal as well as prior performances. This method helps to stimulate teams and drive members towards success.

Online marketers use metrics in order to monitor the number of viewers that land on a website and use this information in comparison to their competitors. Airlines industry often uses its ability to bring in a passenger's luggage to its destination in time and without damages as an encouraging metric to evaluate its baggage handling process. While, a metric frequently used by call centers is to gauge the number of callers that do not connect to a call center agent before hanging up.

Another common tool to measure business process improvement, especially in the manufacturing operations, include statistical methods. Statistical methods determine the crucial process variables, measure the effect of these variables on the process outcome, and improve the outcome by controlling the crucial process variables and permit continuous improvement of the process.

There are two common statistical methods used are- statistical process control (SPC) and statistical quality control (SQC).

SPC/SQC are statistical methods that help companies to develop a better understanding of why problems occur. This allows companies to eliminate the possibility of a problem from occurring, or stopping it before it becomes a real issue.

SPC helps the company to understand whether the process is functioning like it should.

In addition, SPC methods allow companies to track process performance.

SQC refers to statistical quality control and uses statistics to determine the mean, range, measure and common deviation of the business improvement data. This method is used to evaluate problems relating to a product/ service quality and to make the appropriate changes to fix the problem.

The tools used in statistical quality control are beneficial for examining product or service quality. Statistical quality control offers a way to assess problems, get to the root cause of the problem, and ensure high quality products or services and customer satisfaction.

Additionally, all-time favorite metrics used by industries across all verticals include- Sustained growth, Productivity improvement, Cost reduction and Cycle time reduction!

Shruti Bhat

Sustaining operational excellence with the 'new' process

We have come to another important segment of our business process improvement campaign- that is, how to ensure that the success of executing new business process methodology continues to bring in the rewards?

Companies that fail to manage the changes introduced by business process improvement methodologies do not sustain the change for a long time and find themselves reverting to previous routines.

Usually, operationally excellent processes breakdown because:

i.   Employees perceive 'changes' as threats to job security.

ii. Process changes are too frequent.

iii. Change leaders are incompetent or egoist and do not exhibit patience, persuasion and persistence to implement change.

iv. Poor communication.

v.   Very high level of office politics.

vi. Poor employee training.

vii.   No support from organization's top management to bring on a change coupled with wide organizational hierarchy.

viii.   Poor or no follow-up audits, no corrective actions and no preventive actions taken.

Organizations should have appropriate mitigation steps in place to avoid breakdowns due to above risk areas. Personally, I find Kamishibai boards to be a great tool for audit as well as to help sustain operational excellence.

In addition, consistent operational excellence primarily requires (a) Committed and ongoing support from company's senior management and (b) Including the changes into employee's daily routine, timely performance feedback and consistent employee training.

Moreover, organizations should have its employee discipline policy in place. Those who actively prevent operational excellence from happening or maintaining should be strictly dealt with.

Tip: Holding employees accountable is a major contributor to ensure that processes improve over time.

The next logical question is – "Not every business is the same, not every employee maturity level is the same, not every industry vertical is the same- so how do we recommend process improvement methodologies for organizations?"

Process improvement methodology recommendations for different business departments, industry verticals- Coming up!

Methodology recommendations

In this chapter, you will learn- *Recommended business process improvement methodology for:*

- Healthcare organization.

- Facility management of a manufacturing company.

- IT department of manufacturing industries, service organizations, 'non-profits', universities, logistics companies, government offices or Information Technology company.

- Customer service department of a service organization.

It is very pragmatic to use the right tool at the right time.

Coming up in the next chapter- *What is the right process improvement methodology for a Healthcare organization...*

Shruti Bhat

Methodology recommendations for
Healthcare organization.

For Healthcare, the bottom-line is fed from insurance providers and the government. Therefore, if these two are not satisfied, there is no reimbursement, consequently no funds into the hospital. Top reason why hospitals are not reimbursed many a times is too much variation in the hospital administration's business processes. Therefore, the recommended methodology for hospitals is Six Sigma, to control or eliminate variation.

Another 'problem area' in hospital business processes lies in operating rooms, Outpatient departments (OPD), emergency rooms and diagnostic labs.

Operating rooms, OPD, emergency rooms and diagnostic labs are driven by 'flow'. The more number of patients a hospital puts through, the more money the hospital makes and hence thrives. Leaning them provides excess capacity and hence, hospital does not have to spend on new rooms.

Lean, Six Sigma or Lean Six Sigma are recommended methodologies for Healthcare business depending on their underlying problem i.e. poor reimbursements or poor flow management. Additionally, Continuous improvement must be in action, matching pace with flow dynamics, health reform policies and government regulations landscape.

Coming up next, recommended process improvement methodology for *Facility management of a manufacturing facility, university division or a maintenance department...*

Methodology recommendations for Facility management of manufacturing companies

6S and Lean are the best ways to go for a maintenance department / facility management of a manufacturing company, university or a service organization. Reason being 6S methodology gets any department, a facility or a specific area to be able to standardize their inputs and outputs.

Maintenance departments typically have a lot many work orders to their process flow that slows them down. Therefore, simplification through process improvement and standardization by using 6S methodology of Lean will allow them to be more efficient and effective, reduce their operational costs and help them to meet their budgets.

For example- if there were multiple inventories to be sourced to manage these facilities, it would mean managing more suppliers and/ or hiring more people to complete workload i.e. spending more money than required. With inventory standardization, i.e. buying more of the same, cost gets automatically reduced.

Coming up next, recommended process improvement methodology for *IT department of manufacturing industries, service organizations, 'non-profits', universities, logistics companies, government offices or Information Technology company...*

Methodology recommendations for - *IT department of manufacturing industries, service organizations, 'non-profits', universities, logistics companies, government offices or Information Technology company*

Agile, Scrum and Quality-by design (QbD) are proven process improvement methodologies for IT companies as well as IT departments of manufacturing & service organizations, non-profits, hospitals, universities, government offices etc.

An IT department's function within an enterprise usually involves making sure computers are processing what they need to process, the website, internet are up and running, support HR and finance divisions, approve software needed by their team or other departments within the organization.

The IT companies manage digital cloud; develop software programs for logistics, inventory management, games, social media, finance, anti-virus & security systems, messaging and other telecommunications apps etc.

Most technology companies exist in fast-paced environment and they employ knowledgeable design engineers, developers. If they have a clear understanding of customer requirements, then these engineers can design and development almost anything. Agile and Scrum process improvement methodologies bring design engineers closer to the customer.

Combining Agile/ Scrum with Quality by design further brings these design experts closer to the customer viewpoint. Voice of the customer is clearly understood. In addition, these methodologies facilitate a standard process for designing and developing products. This could lead to process innovation and not just product innovation, because the developers might find things that one can design that might change the very process!

Another big cause of failures within Technology companies is not understanding their large classification of customers i.e. not just users, but everyone around their product. For example-Discrepancies in service level agreements with both users and vendors. In such incidences, Six Sigma may be helpful, although, Agile and Scrum sort out such discrepancies too.

Coming up next, recommended process improvement methodology for- *Customer service department of a service organization (for example-hotel industry, tourism industry, call centers, retail business, car rental companies, banks and financial institutions, realtor business etc.) ...*

Methodology recommendations for *Customer service department of a service organization*

Six Sigma is a proven methodology for improving profitability and performance of customer service department for example- hotel industry, tourism industry, call centers, retail business, car rental companies, banks and financial institutions, realtor business etc.

Customer service departments handle inquires, they interact with customers for either new business or to service their current business or complaints that are coming in.

Good customer service happens when the very cause(s) of customer dis-satisfaction are eliminated.

The way to go for such organizations would be to make an exhaustive list of- what are the reasons that make their customers mad in the first place. Minimize or eliminate those causes. Then, focus on ways to selling more business.

A frequent question that arises during 'process improvement' methodology selection meetings is- Can a company choose one improvement methodology and then move on to another process improvement methodology later?

My response to this is 'Yes'. The reason being- business operating systems will morph and change back. Therefore, the tools have to change too.

There is evolutionary maturity too i.e. a company might start with something simple and advance later.

Selection of 'business process improvement' methodology stems out of business strategies. As the business evolves, goals change and therefore strategies change. Process improvement methodology thus, has to change as needed to meet business goals.

Goals change every 3-5 years, therefore, process improvement methodology has to adapt either to this change or in cases where it is not possible to modify prevailing methodology, a new methodology may be needed altogether.

The key is to evolve business operating systems to match what the business needs to support the customers at that time.

The up-coming chapter addresses few frequently asked questions on Business process improvement and Continuous improvement...

Frequently asked questions

FAQ 1

Is it BPI or BPR- What is the difference between Business Process Improvement and Business Process Re-engineering?

Response: A business process defines the various activities involved in achieving a particular goal. Business processes briefly describe the chain of events that are involved in an activity or a group of activities such as- running a business, manufacturing of products or selling products or services.

Business Process Improvement (BPI) and Business Process Re-engineering (BPR) are two widely used terms while attempting to modify business processes in order for organizations to sustain and grow.

As the name implies, both BPI and BPR deal with business process modification, however, they are two widely different terms. Allow me to ask few questions to explain these terms:

- Is your process broken?
- Does it have a high impact on your company's strategic direction?
- Is it antiquated?

83

- Does it fall far below 'best-in-class' or desired 'state-of-the-art'?

If your answer to the above questions is 'Yes', then its BPR, meaning- those said processes have to be re-engineered or re-designed. BPR technique assumes that the current process is irrelevant, does not work and therefore needs overhauling completely from A to Zee.

For all those business processes that do not need re-engineering, but essentially need modification for benefiting the business, it is BPI - business process improvement.

FAQ 2

Can you throw some light on E-business process improvement?

Response: It is no secret that the internet plays a vital role in many businesses. Enhancements to business interactions become easier through the internet and allow handling of business relationships in a different way than before.

E-business describes the combination of an organization's informative and communicative tools, technologies, otherwise known as "business software". It allows for the improvement of processes by creating more value to the organization, clients and associates.

E-business is not only applicable to companies that exists virtually, but incorporates all types of businesses. The desired result of e-business process management is to complete processes in a quicker manner, while spending less money and adding value to the company. Often, creating value brings forth an increase in motivation amongst employees, overall satisfaction of customers, a rise in profit margins and favored affiliations with associates.

E-business process improvement aims to lower mistakes caused by individuals because of misunderstandings or miscommunications, while

85

motivating participants towards their role requirements.

Be it a brick and mortar workplace or an e-business, both need to stay in business to sustain and grow. The problems faced by brick & mortar and e- businesses are not same. However, there are quite a few 'similar' problems. E- business process improvement methodologies must be appropriately selected, enforced, monitored and continued for business efficiency, sustained growth and consistent increasing profits.

The process of selecting business improvement methodology remains the same for brick and mortar as well as e-businesses.

FAQ 3

Is Six Sigma the ultimate business process improvement methodology?

Response: There is no ultimate business improvement management method.

Over the years, several business process improvement methodologies have been suggested and successfully applied to various industry sectors. My book entitled "Business Process Improvement for Manufacturing and Service Industry" cites 18 such methodologies.

Built upon each other, these methodologies often employ common tools for problem solving. They represent the experiences and thoughts about process improvement by workers, managers, consultants, and scholars throughout the entire industrial age. Business process improvement methodologies are still evolving today, as more and more organizations have started to implement them.

None of the process improvement methods, including Six Sigma is ultimate.

FAQ 4

In how many cases do you do a pre - assessment before starting a project?

Response: For every business improvement project, irrespective of its size, time invested through pre-assessment will go a long way towards avoiding projects, which actually should not have started and succeeding in the one that you do need to start.

One of the services I offer in my consulting practice is business assessment. This initiates a project in 85 to 90% of my engagements and charters the problem areas with priority, scope, deliverables, approximations of timelines and cost.

To meet success with business improvement initiatives, one has to seek answers to following basic questions-

iv.   What is the 'change' objective we are trying to achieve?

v.   How are we measuring the 'change' i.e. how will we know that a 'change' is an 'improvement'?

vi.   What 'changes' should we make that will result in an 'improvement'?

vii.   A strategic and structured pre-assessment finds true answers to all of the above questions effectively.

FAQ 5

For continuous improvement to be effective, do you; need big data or lean data?

Response: Too much and unnecessary data gets confusing, leads to analysis-paralysis and in fact, is counterproductive. Type and extent of data collected, should be explicitly defined before collection, in order for it to remain lean.

FAQ 6

What are the top technical and people skills to look for while hiring Continuous Improvement or BPM experts or a Management Consulting firm?

Response: There are nine skills of highly effective Continuous Improvement/ Business Process Management Experts, namely:

1. Ability to understand client's business and be efficient at stakeholder management.

2. Should have an integrated and overall understanding of the industry sector, its verticals, peculiarities, regulations & legislations, product types, customer avenues and marketing geographies. Most importantly for companies, it is imperative to match 'chemistry' with the expert rather than looking at 'geometry' of the consulting firm.

3. Up-to-date knowledge of different continuous improvement / business process management methodologies.

4. Passion for implementing them in order to bring forth the desired positive changes within prescribed time, scope and budget.

5. Ability to speak up when top management is wrong.

6. Ability to explain complex ideas in simple words.

7. Ability to listen and openness to learning.

8. Patience, persistence and persuasion while bringing on and/or managing change.

9. *Amnesia-* This is the most vital criteria. The continuous improvement expert should forget all the good work he/she did with previous organizations- What worked there may not work in the new place, as each company has its own set of business processes, people, organizational culture, office politics and associated problems as a result thereof. The continuous improvement expert should have a mindset of always 'starting with a clean slate'.

Conclusion

Another common question posed to me is *"What is the ultimate business process improvement method?"*

My response is- There is no ultimate business improvement management method. Please do not waste your time to search for one.

No matter what name a method has and what benefits it claims that it can generate, it will never be the only solution to improve the organizational performance or competitiveness.

Over-commitment to it may actually weaken an organization's competitive advantage. To grow, an organization must balance process improvement with other initiatives such as innovation, improved product/ service features, employee development.

Although process improvement is able to improve lead-time, productivity, inventories, cost, and quality, it can never replace an innovative product.

In other words, a new product needed and wanted by customers will generate a dramatic demand in the marketplace that the organization can succeed even without process improvement. Having said that, *if such a customer centric innovative company were to follow 'continuous business process improvement' technique, it would further augment its profits.*

We have come towards the end of this book. A parting message- The impressions, protocols, steps, matrices, models, metrics presented in this book have been successfully implemented, hands-on. I hope you find them useful and wish you all, the very best in your campaign with business process improvement.

The secret of change is to focus all of your energy, not on fighting the old, but on building the new.

- Socrates

Other publications by the author

Business Process Improvement for Manufacturing and Service Industry

This book presents practical ways to build and improve business processes and assists professionals whether they are learning the basics of business process improvement (or Continuous improvement), planning their first improvement project, or evangelizing process oriented thinking throughout their organization.

This book is for Agile entrepreneurs, Startups, Leaders, QA (Quality Assurance) managers, Management consulting professionals, Production supervisors, Manufacturing heads, CEOs, Directors and Managers involved in decision-making, directing their organization's sustainability, profitability and expansion.

If you want some new and effective ideas for improving your organization's efficiency, then this self-help business management book is for you.

This book is also for professionals who are interested in making a career change and wish to embrace business process management (bpm) role. This book simplifies 18 most promising business improvement methodologies, which would help executives, management consultants, improve organizational performance in their new role as a Business Analyst, Continuous Improvement or Process Management Expert.

Sample Chapter:

Introduction- What is a business process?

One of the first people to describe business processes was Adam Smith (1776) in his famous example of a pin factory. Since then business processes have evolved and better defined. A business process defines the various activities involved in achieving a particular goal. Business processes briefly describe the chain of events that are involved in an activity or a group of activities. It is common to use a business process if the activities influence current products or data and bring about production.

Types of business processes include-

- Management processes such as Corporate governance, Strategic management, planning and implementation.

- Operational processes, which constitute the core business and create primary value stream. Typically, they include Procurement & sourcing, Manufacturing, Marketing, Sales and Customer service.

- Supporting processes, which support the operational processes and include Finance & Accounting, Recruitment & Human Resources Management, Research and Technical support.

Some examples include invoicing, product shipping details, updating information, tracking orders, allocating budgets etc. Business processes used throughout organization, at any level, are outlined in order to improve organization in an effective and efficient way.

There can be several inputs in a business process but there is always only one output or specific goal- that is to help business thrive.

Business processes are used practically in any organization and throughout an organization at any level. They are used in a variety of industries such as private, public sector, government, departments, hospitals, charities etc. Business processes are, typically outlined in order to improve an organization in an effective and efficient way.

Various computer software make it possible to create business processes on a computer, however simple business processes are just as effective when written with pen and paper. Some even find it better to jot down the processes on a piece of paper, or on several small ones, to kick start their creativity and thinking process. It is up to the professional (and/or organization) to decide whether a software or traditional method will work best for them.

Business processes work best when there is input, support and ideas from various people that are involved in the organization (or department).

Key business processes are logically grouped related tasks and activities, independent of the organization's structure, which utilize the resources of the organization to produce specific results. They possess measurable inputs & outputs, value addition and repeatable activity.

Tip- The effective management of key business process requires- Ownership & planning, performance metrics & control, process qualification, management and improvement methodology.

A business process *always* begins with a customer's need and ends with a customer's need fulfilment.

Customer needs change, technologies change, government policies change, competition changes and what used to be a high level of performance becomes a poor one and it's time to replace the formerly good process with a new one-only every process cycle should have this capacity of identification, in-built in its charter.

As a Business Transformation expert of many years, I am happy to mention here few case studies, nay success stories. Let me share three examples-

A consumer goods manufacturing company redesigned its product deployment process, by means of which, it now manufactures goods and delivers them to its distribution center such that inventory uptake was reduced by 35%, while stock-out goods situation declined by 70%.

A pharmaceutical company created a new product development process, which reduced time to market by 75%, development costs by 45% and increased productivity by 30%.

An engineering goods manufacturing organization increased its product delivery targets by 350% and reduced its supply chain costs by up to 55%. Something to note in these is [...]

End of this sample book. Enjoyed the preview?

Checkout the book at
http://www.fastread.ca/business-process-improvement-for-manufacturing-and-service-industry.html

Kaizen for

Pharmaceutical,
Medical Device &
Biotech Industries

DR. SHRUTI BHAT, PhD, MBA
Certified Lean Six Sigma Black Belt

Business Process Management Systems and Continuous Improvement
Executive Guide Series

Kaizen for Pharmaceutical, Medical Device & Biotech Industries as Paperback and Digital editions.

Kaizen procedures evolved in the automobile industry. Therefore, most of Kaizen literature, publications, books, cite Kaizen implementation in factories such as Toyota, Ford, Mazda and the like. But work practices within pharmaceutical, medical device and biotech industry are different from the auto sector.

This book also provides a structured approach to designing Kaizen strategies, practices and implementation for pharmaceutical, medical device and biotech companies.

This book will be most applicable to small to medium-size companies. It will demystify Kaizen and help business leaders in pharmaceutical, medical device, biotech and all life sciences organizations, irrespective of their size or workplace culture.

It will also provide practical and useful examples and case studies of Kaizen principles that can be executed at various levels across the organization as well as for yourself as an individual to further your personal career.

And last but not the least, it will help to improve revenues and create a lasting profitable change by using Kaizen principles and techniques.

If you want some new ideas for exponentially improving your business, make increase in R&D efficiency, productivity and need to get your team involved then this business management book is for you.

Sample Chapter:

Preface

A few years ago, I was approached by a CEO of a pharmaceutical contract research company to turnaround his sick unit into a profitable enterprise. This company was dealing with the the development of solid oral dosage forms.

To bring about the necessary change, we initiated several Kaizen campaigns companywide, with 360 degrees focus to overhaul all processes and operational systems.

We addressed all key areas across the organization including accounts payable/receivable, material procurement, order processing, suppliers, R&D, scale-up, production, logistics, product dossiers filings, project management, business development, sales & marketing and PR communication processes.

Another key area where Kaizen helped us in a big way was to integrate various client information data sets maintained within different databases on separate systems.

Before Kaizen, everything was disjointed, delayed and everyone was working in silos, leading to waste and lost revenues.

Post Kaizen, there was teamwork
and excellent cash-flow!

At the end of nine months, this company's books started showing profits, and from there on, it kept going from 'good to great'. It was an excellent example of a successful transformation.

Unfortunately, this contract research company is not alone in the challenges it has faced. Studies indicate that 88% of business owners in North America struggle to maintain consistent cash-flow. Key questions to consider are:

- Can your organization benefit from increased workplace productivity?

- Does your team face challenges with reduced R&D budget?

- Does your organization face challenges because of inconsistent or poor cash-flow?

- Do you need to cut corners as you are forced to do more with less?

If you answered 'yes' to any of the above questions, then Kaizen should be your mantra...

Kaizen is an outstanding business tool that helps organizations to achieve new heights!

Kaizen procedures evolved in the automobile industry. Therefore, most of Kaizen literature, publications, books, cite Kaizen implementation in factories such as Toyota, Ford, Mazda and the like. But work practices within pharmaceutical (medical device and biotech) industry are different from the auto sector.

Regulations, customer demands, competitor landscape, product criteria, facility and environmental needs, employee skills within pharmaceutical (medical devices and biotech) companies are extremely stringent and totally different from the automobile industry. Therefore, 'as is' Kaizen practices from auto sector won't work for pharmaceutical, medical device, and biotech organizations. Kaizen must be customized for these industries, to achieve its full benefits.

So far, there has been no book on Kaizen that is customized to pharmaceutical, medical device, and biotech industries.

Having successfully driven more than 250 Kaizen, Lean Six Sigma, and other continuous improvement projects within pharmaceuticals, NHP, medical devices, biotech and healthcare sectors, worldwide for over a decade, I have created real success stories; I felt it will be beneficial to share those techniques and experiences.

This book is a structured approach to designing Kaizen strategies, practices and implementation for pharmaceutical, medical device, and biotech companies.

It is an invaluable resource, an essential tool for all professionals within the pharmaceutical, medical device, biotech organizations i.e. all life sciences and health care companies, interested in employing Kaizen in their workplaces and their personal lives.

This book will also facilitate running Kaizen in a manufacturing company and do it at a world-class level.

Get ahead with product innovations, improved laboratory productivity, first to file, increased intellectual property, efficient manufacturing, effective marketing and logistics with KAIZEN.

This book doesn't simply explain Kaizen process features, implementation, and application. The scope of this book is much wide.

This book is meant for small to medium-size pharmaceutical, medical device and biotech research, manufacturing and contract services companies.

This book is to-

- Demystify Kaizen and help business leaders in pharmaceutical, medical device, biotech, and all life sciences organizations, irrespective of their size or workplace culture.

- Apply Kaizen to what really matters, that is, 'to achieve business expansion along with increased productivity and profits'.

- Provide practical and useful examples of Kaizen principles that can be executed at various levels: across the organization; within a specific department, business unit or team, as well as for yourself as an individual to further your personal career.

- Improve revenues and create a lasting change using Kaizen principles and techniques.

Kaizen requires very less investment, therefore can be implemented to its full potential even in startups.

Some salient features of this book

- It shows pharmaceutical & biotech scientists, design engineers, operators and everyone involved in product development, how to utilize Kaizen- to create innovations, shorten product development times, improve first-to-file rates, conduct successful scale-up and technology transfer to manufacturing sites.

- It shows everyone associated with manufacturing, how to use Kaizen to decrease cycle times, work-in-process & quarantine inventories, the cost of distribution & logistics, improve equipment efficiency, facility capacity utilization and shift output.

- It shows everyone in Human Resources how to use Kaizen to minimize employee turnover, hire and retain talent, and motivate employees to create a difference.

- It shows the company's senior management, stakeholders, finance and other supporting business units, how to use Kaizen to increase ROI (return on investment) while complying with cGMP (*current* Good Manufacturing Practices) and other regulations, address rising competition and counteract fluctuating market economy.

- This book presents useful ideas that one can implement immediately, often at no additional cost.

- It shows how to transform a business from 'good- to- great'. True benefits of Kaizen implementation are realized because, it adds value to your products, increases market share, and drives both top line and bottom line of your business.

Kaizen has mainly been used in Japan and many other SE Asian companies and in Europe. Up until now, it has not gained enough significance in North America, because of which it has not been utilized to its full potential.

The root cause is the difference in work culture and corporate governance styles of companies in eastern and western countries; this book totally eliminates this gap.

This book presents Kaizen methodology for direct implementation within a pharmaceutical, medical device, biotech company in east or west.

Moreover, this book helps you to customize Kaizen to your company; this book is not a 'vanilla generic'.

In addition, this book is an excellent resource for Kaizen beginners with a lot of real life industry examples, case studies and provides several 'do-it-yourself' exercises, which is of tremendous value, in absence of a Kaizen coach […]

Kaizen is not just to 'SAVE' more

…

Kaizen helps to 'MAKE' more-MORE products, more customers, more revenues …

End of this sample book. Enjoyed the preview?

Checkout the book at
http://www.fastread.ca/business-books-blog/kaizen-for-pharmaceutical-medical-device-biotech-industries

Kaizen: How to use Kaizen for increased profitability and organizational excellence.

Kaizen principles have been viewed as one of the key factors to Japanese competitiveness. This book presents a practical way to build and improve business processes, and assists professionals whether they are learning the basics of business process improvement, planning their first improvement project, or evangelizing process oriented thinking throughout their organization.

This book is for Agile entrepreneurs, Leaders, QA (Quality Assurance) managers, Management consulting professionals, Production supervisors, Manufacturing heads, CEOs, Directors and all Managers involved in decision-making, directing their organization's sustainability, profitability, and expansion.

If you want some new ideas for improving your business and need to get your team involved then this concise self-help, business management book is for you.

This book is also for professionals who are interested in making a career change and wish to embrace business process management (bpm) role.

This book simplifies Kaizen continuous improvement methodology, which would help executives; change management professionals improve business situations in their new role as a Business Analyst, Process Improvement, or Process Management Expert.

This book is also for graduate students, budding out of colleges and are in the process of stepping into the industrial world- be it manufacturing or a service industry. This book helps them learn Kaizen ways to improve their company's business, which in turn would help their career growths.

Lastly, but not the least, this book is for "all business readers" who wish to apply business improvement methodologies to their work place in most beneficial and practical ways.

Sample Chapter

Introduction

The term Kaizen come from a Japanese phrase that means 'Make Better'. It uses the Japanese judgment of improving the workplace internally to bring about desired results.

The Kaizen institute defines 'Kaizen' as the Japanese term for continuous improvement. It uses common sense, statistical quality control and an adaptive framework of organizational values and beliefs, which keeps workers and management focussed on zero defects. It is a philosophy of never being satisfied with what has been accomplished, but to keep improvement on-going.

Improvements through Kaizen have a focus. Kaizen generates process-oriented thinking is people-oriented and is directed at people's efforts. Rather than identifying employees as the 'problem', Kaizen emphasizes that the 'process' is the 'target' and employees can provide improvements by understanding how their joint fits into the process and changing it.

The essence of Kaizen is that, people that perform a certain task are most knowledgeable about that task; consequently, by involving them and showing confidence in their capabilities, ownership of the process is raised to its highest level. In addition, the team effort encourages innovation and change and by involving all layers of employees, the imaginary organizational walls disappear to make room for productive improvements. From such a perspective,

Kaizen is not only an approach to manufacturing competitiveness, but also everybody's business, because its premise is based on the concept that every person has an interest in improvement.

The roots of Kaizen reach back to the late 1940s, when Japan's economy was still reeling from the second World War.

Kaizen principles have been viewed as one of the key factors to Japanese competitiveness. It begins with the admission that every organization has problems, which provide opportunities for change. It evolves around involving everyone in the organization and largely depends on cross-functional teams that can be empowered to challenge the status quo.

Working with Deming and other consultants, Japanese industries created several new management approaches, one of which was Kaizen. Using these approaches, they were soon able to out-produce their counterparts in other industrial nations, and earn a reputation for quality and economy. Today, Japan is a world leader in auto and electronics manufacturing!

Kaizen techniques became famous when Toyota used them to rise to world's automotive leadership. The company is credited as pioneer to formalize Kaizen technique and implement it as part of a global business plan. Rather than undertake large projects, Toyota's staff was encouraged to identify problems, no matter how small, trace their root causes and implement all necessary solutions.

Over a single year, one of Toyota's plants in the United States recorded over 75,000 suggestions from 7,000 employees, and reported implementing over 99% of those suggestions.

Every implemented step had a positive effect on safety, efficiency, productivity, and/or reliability. While each step may have been small on its own, the total result was a drastic and long-lasting improvement in the company.

That's the drive of Kaizen — many small steps, all in the right direction, continuing indefinitely.

Since Kaizen comes from the words, "Renew the heart and make it good." Therefore, adaptation of the Kaizen concept also requires changes in "the heart of the business", corporate culture and structure, since Kaizen enables companies to translate the corporate vision in every aspect of a company's operational practice.

Kaizen Philosophy: 3 pillars of Kaizen

- Housekeeping.

- Waste elimination.

- Standardization.

The House of Kaizen stays on three pillars- good housekeeping, effective waste-elimination and efficient standardization of work. These pillars are cemented strong with 3 factors- visual management, Kaizen leader and Kaizen training. This 3x3 formula is a basic necessity for success with Kaizen.

The Kaizen philosophy was developed to improve manufacturing processes, and it is one of the elements which led to the success of Japanese manufacturing through high quality and low costs. However, one can gain the benefits of the Kaizen approach in many other working environments too, and both at personal level or for a whole team or organization.

Kaizen philosophy:

- With Kaizen, some of the common elements of business philosophy change drastically.

- Managers see how things are done, organize, and implement changes.

- Employees are expected to offer improvements to procedures.

- Innovation can come from anyone with an idea.

- Final quality comes from attention at every step of production.

- Reliability comes from good maintenance processes.

- Inventory levels are kept small to reduce waste. Production problems must be caught and resolved before a shortage arises.

- Specialization is useful, but understanding "before" and "after" gives extra insight (making each employee that much more valuable).

- Changes to the system are made constantly, in small steps, at every level of the company, to achieve ongoing improvement.

Tip: The message of Kaizen philosophy is that, not one single day should go by without some type of improvement being made, in some process, in the company.

Tip: Kaizen is everyone's job. The Kaizen approach requires that all employees participate; therefore, everyone in the company is encouraged to play a role in Kaizen activities.

Kaizen has three major components:

1. Perceptiveness- All Kaizen projects are based on identified problems. If no problem has been identified, there is no Kaizen.
2. Idea generation.
3. Decision implementation, monitoring and evaluation.

Much of the focus in Kaizen is on reducing "waste" and this waste takes EIGHT forms:

1. Mistakes/Reworks.

2. Excess Inventory (includes material, time and information).

3. Transporting (Unnecessary Transport of Materials).

4. Motion (Unnecessary Movement of People).

5. Waiting (or delays).

6. Over Processing (Excess Process Steps).

7. Over Producing (Services/Goods do not meet the Customer demands).

8. Failure to Utilize the Time and/or Staff Talents.

Kaizen creates a constant flow of facility-improving ideas. Many of these ideas would never be shared, and would never be implemented, without Kaizen.

Each new idea is a small step in the right direction — part of the continuing process of improvement. Over time, these numerous small steps add up to provide substantial benefits to the facility.

As for the bottom line- steadily improving on efficiency and quality make organizations more successful [...]

End of this sample book. Enjoyed the preview?

Checkout the book at
http://www.fastread.ca/kaizen-tabh-academy.html

Continuous Improvement- 30 Proven Tools to Drive Profitability, Quality and Operational Effectiveness in Manufacturing & Service Industry

Businesses however big or small, can only sustain if they adapt themselves to changing market dynamics, economic seesaw and customer demands. This, very sustenance is affected by five main factors namely- people, money, machines, processes and materials. Processes being the most critical factor, which the author terms as 'Business Lifeline'.

Therefore, for a business to survive and grow, their business processes must evolve appropriately to make running the business both affordable and profitable. This constant adaption is brought about by Continuous improvement.

This book provides deep insights into thirty vital tools necessary to meet success with Continuous improvement campaigns. This book helps you learn the various methods by which you can improve your company's business processes, which in turn would help your individual career growth.

This book simplifies business improvement methodologies, gives sequential steps to facilitate selecting a business process improvement, which is right for your organization, helps you understand the principles that drive business improvement and give your career the boost it needs!

This book is for Agile entrepreneurs, Startups, Leaders, QA (Quality Assurance) managers, Management consulting professionals, Production supervisors, Project leaders, Manufacturing heads, CEOs, Directors and Managers involved in decision-making, and in directing their organization's sustainability, profitability, and expansion.

This book is also for professionals who are interested in making a career change and wish to embrace business process management (bpm) role.

This book also helps executive professionals improve organizational performance in their role as a Management Consultant, Business Analyst, Continuous Improvement, or Process Management Expert.

Check out the book at:

http://www.fastread.ca/30-proven-tools-continuous-improvement.html

Modular Kaizen Vs Kaizen Blitz: How to choose between these two Kaizen Business Process Improvement methodologies for accelerated productivity, profitability and organizational excellence.

Sample Chapter

Introduction

The starting point for improvement is to recognize 'the need'. Kaizen principles emphasize problem-awareness and provide clues to identifying problems. Once identified, problems must be solved. Therefore, Kaizen is also a problem-solving process. But, most of all, Kaizen is a management philosophy that forces higher standards at all levels of the organization by encouraging continuous improvement in all processes- Kaizen is dual in nature.

Duality of Kaizen

Kaizen is intrinsically dual in nature. It is a union of 'Kaizen Philosophy' and 'Kaizen Action Plan'.

- As a philosophy, Kaizen is about developing organizational excellence by creating awareness. It is all about building a company-wide culture where all employees, senior management, and stakeholders are actively engaged in identifying and ideating ways of improving the business's performance, operations and processes.

- As an action plan, Kaizen is about organizing Kaizen events, workshops, action force and focus groups, dedicated to ideate and implement improvement plans to the company's existing processes, to make them better. Kaizen events are run by employee teams from all levels of the company, especially those most close to the process (being considered for improvement).

Kaizen has various formats- Lean Kaizen, Gemba Kaizen, Modular Kaizen, Blitz Kaizen, Process Kaizen, Flow Kaizen, Agile Kaizen, Daily Kaizen.

Gemba Kaizen, Process Kaizen, Flow Kaizen comprise 'Kaizen Philosophies', while Lean Kaizen, Modular Kaizen, Agile Kaizen, Daily Kaizen and Blitz Kaizen are 'Kaizen Action Plan' to take a company from being Good-to-Great!

Do you want to initiate Kaizen in your organization? *As it is said, every big achievement begins with a small step.*

End of this sample whitepaper. Enjoyed the preview?

Checkout the book at https://www.amazon.com/dp/B071Z2QW 3L/ref=sr_1_2?ie=UTF8&qid=1494547014 &sr=8-2&keywords=shruti+bhat

Let us continue the discussion

It does not have to stop with this eBook... Let us work together!

Schedule Dr. Shruti Bhat for a keynote speech, breakout, seminar, workshop or webinar in order to help your employees or association members do more business and be more successful!

Write to http://www.drshrutibhat.com/contact.html Contact Ana Anderson for details.

Training course

Are you frustrated with delays in new product development?

Are you frustrated with mounting expenses in your company and wish to control costs?

Do you wish to improve productivity in manufacturing?

Do you wish to increase customer satisfaction?

Grab this exclusive course and learn- *How to continuously improve operational excellence?*

How to Continuously Improve Operational Excellence?

In this course, you will learn-

1. How to identify the business problem?
2. Ten tools of identifying a business problem.
3. How to do business process mapping effectively?
4. How to apply business process improvement to R&D, Operations, Logistics and Quality departments of your organization to improve Innovation, Production, Distribution Operations & Quality.

5. Different avenues to cut costs (without compromising quality).
6. How to improve productivity and customer satisfaction?
7. How to become a customer centric company and make profits exponentially?

This web-based, self-paced training is brought to you by Innoworks Institute Canada, only for $349. Includes: 9 audio/ video masterclasses and 6 printable PDF course books. Plus, free action guides, worksheets, teleconsultation and much more!

Reach Helpdesk at

http://www.innoworks.ca/training.html to get a free detailed brochure about this exclusive course! Mention passcode 'BPM#2146' to avail a 10% discount on course enrollment! *Hurry enroll now.*

FREE GIFT

And before we close, we would like to offer you a free gift. You can download a copy of Dr. Shruti Bhat's FAQ Gold Sheet - Answers for 25 frequently asked questions on Business Process Management absolutely **FREE** from her website.

This book has been presented by…

ShiftingParadigms

Printed in Great Britain
by Amazon